CW01664940

Coming, Ready or Not!

All-age Services for Advent to Epiphany

Val Hawthorne

kevin mayhew

kevin
mayhew

First published in Great Britain in 2011 by Kevin Mayhew Ltd
Buxhall, Stowmarket, Suffolk IP14 3BW
Tel: +44 (0) 1449 737978 Fax: +44 (0) 1449 737834
E-mail: info@kevinmayhewltd.com

www.kevinmayhew.com

ISBN 978 1 84867 395 3
Catalogue No. 1501281

Cover design by Rob Mortonson
© Image used under licence from Shutterstock Inc.

Project managed by Free Range Book Design & Production

Printed and bound in Great Britain

Contents

About the author

Val Hawthorne is a musician and former teacher who has been involved in the life of the Church for more years than she cares to remember. She has sung in and conducted adult choirs as well as church choirs, music groups and worship teams. She has composed musicals and songs for children and Bible-based assemblies. More recently Val has written books that help children to pray and resources for Church services. Val likes to write songs that are lively and fun as well as thoughtful music with a message. Most of all she seeks to bring the Bible to life for children and make worship meaningful and accessible in a family church. Any spare time is taken up with her grandchildren!

Other books by Val Hawthorne
All Together Worship (1501162)
Sing the Christmas Story (1450345)
All About a Baby (1501229)
The Gift Bringer (1450400)
The Christmas Dream (1450424)

Introduction

Advent	a time of hope; of light shining in darkness; of wonder and mystery.
Christmas	a time of joy and celebration at the birth of our Saviour.
Epiphany	a time of revelation and of looking ahead in the light of his birth.

The services in this book celebrate this special time from Advent to Epiphany. Prophetic words and familiar stories, songs and carols, prayers and readings are all presented in an informal and accessible way. They are services appropriate for all-age worship. If yours, like mine, is a family church where there are babies and great-grandmothers and everyone in-between, then hopefully this book will be a useful resource for you to draw on.

Some of the services offer opportunity for outreach: the second Sunday in Advent is a time to invite those who have recently been bereaved, while Christmas Eve is an occasion for all the family and their friends. Why not send out invitations to those who have been married in your church or had their children baptised there?

Each service follows a similar pattern, with something to engage the children but with content suitable for adults as well. The hymns and songs I suggest are a mix of traditional, contemporary and child-friendly. The usual times for confession, prayers, seasonal collects and a statement of faith are included.

Props may be required for the children's activity and you will need to ask other people to be involved in various ways. Some responsorial prayers are used and these will either need to be on a service sheet or on a screen, using powerpoint or an overhead projector.

The framework allows scope for you to adapt it to your particular congregation and situation. Each service lasts for approximately an hour.

I hope you will find this book both helpful and enjoyable as you seek to bring this hope, joy and revelation to your church.

Val Hawthorne

Advent one

Coming, ready or not!

Have an Advent wreath or crown ready at the front of the church with a suitable lighter. Choose someone before the service to be the 'seeker' in the game. Have three people prepared to read the Light of the World prayers and two readers. If you wish you can put on a wedding hat or buttonhole for the talk or involve children in taking part by dressing a bride and having a groom walk down the church to meet her.

Welcome

Good morning everybody and welcome to our service today. Happy New Year!

That's a strange thing to say at the beginning of December isn't it? We say Happy New Year on January the first, don't we? But it is the start of a new year. Today is Advent Sunday and Advent Sunday is the first Sunday in the Church calendar. Maybe we should say, 'Happy New Church Year'.

Let's all stand up and greet each other and say together, 'Happy New Church Year!'

Now please sit. We have something special here for Advent. It is our Advent wreath *(crown if you prefer)*. You can see it is a circle of greenery. The circle symbolises the eternal, never-ending love of God.

There are four candles set in the circle – one for each Sunday in this time of Advent that will take us to Christmas Day. In the middle is the special, big candle to be lit on Christmas Day. So today we'll light our first candle. *(Choose someone to light the candle.)*

In Advent we think about light coming in darkness. Jesus is the Light of the World and as we come together to worship this morning to think about the wonder and mystery of Advent we sing our first song.

Song Light of the world, you stepped down into darkness *or* All earth was dark (Lights to the world) *or* Immortal, invisible, God only wise

Prayer We come here today in hope and expectation. Be with us, Lord, as we look forward to your coming. In our joy and excitement let us not forget the times we fail and do wrong and need to ask forgiveness.

Confession Advent is a time of light shining in darkness. It is a time of new beginnings. Let us spend a few moments looking into the dark corners of our own hearts and ask that the light of Jesus will shine into them.

(Pause.)

Jesus Christ, Light of the World,
scatter the darkness from about us and within us
and help us to walk as children of the light.
Help us to know that you love us
and are with us always.

David Adam

We pray for God's forgiveness for those times when we fail him.

Holy and ever-loving God,
we thank you for the forgiveness of sins
and the opportunities to start anew.
We pray that you will fill our hearts with your goodness
and our minds with your love.

David Adam

Absolution

May Almighty God,
who sent his Son into the world to save sinners,
bring you his pardon and peace, now and for ever.
Amen.

New Patterns for Worship

Activity

Who likes playing games? A game *(my)* lots of children like to play is Hide and Seek. Put up your hand if you have ever played Hide and Seek. I think that's pretty well everybody. We all know the rules, don't we? Someone – the seeker – closes their eyes and counts to 50 or 100 while everyone else hides. When they've finished counting they shout 'Coming, ready or not!' Then they go and find everyone.

We'll play a little game of Hide and Seek now. Here's our seeker and let's have a few people to hide *(choose 3 or 4 children).*

Our seeker is only going to count to 10 today and then she'll shout 'Coming, ready or not!'

Right, seeker – close your eyes and slowly count to 10. Off you go hiders!

'Coming, ready or not!'

(Seeker finds the children who are hiding.)

Well done everyone.

(Children go back to their seats.)

Coming, ready or not. Advent is all about someone coming. In fact the word 'advent' means 'coming'. *(Ask the children)* So who is coming? (Jesus.) When is Jesus coming? (At Christmas.)

Yes, we think of Jesus coming at Christmas – being born in that stable in Bethlehem. But Advent is also about another coming. It is about the time when Jesus will come again here on earth. Will we be ready for him?

Before we think some more about this second coming we'll stand and sing again.

Song Come, thou long-expected Jesus *or* When he comes *or* Soon and very soon

Readings We're going to listen to some verses from the Bible now.

Reader one

Keep awake therefore, for you do not know on what day your Lord will come. But understand this: If the owner of the house had known in what part of the night the thief was coming, he would have stayed awake and not let his house be broken into. Therefore you also must be ready, for the Son of Man is coming at an unexpected time.

Matthew 24:42-44 (NRSV)

Reader two

But about that day or hour no one knows, neither the angels in heaven, nor the Son but only the Father. Beware, keep alert, for you do not know when the time will come . . . keep awake – for you do not know when the master of the house will come, in the evening, or at midnight or at cockcrow or at dawn, or else he may find you asleep when he comes suddenly.

And what I say to you all: keep awake.

Mark 13:32, 33, 35, 37 (NRSV)

Talk I wonder how many times someone has said to you, 'Are you ready?' and then probably, 'Come on, hurry up. It's time to go.' Are you ready? It's time.

Over the next few weeks I expect you will be getting ready for Christmas in your home. It's a very busy time: cards to write; food to prepare; presents to wrap; and all that shopping! So much to do. Will we ever be ready? Well, whether we are ready or not, Christmas will come.

In our readings we heard Jesus telling us to be ready. Ready for what? Listen to this story that Jesus told. It's about a wedding. Who's been to a wedding? Who's organised a wedding? Oh my, what a lot of work that is! So much to think of – so much to do and prepare. Anyone who has planned one will know. First you have to decide the date; then the place and the time. That's just the beginning. Then you get on to the really important things – like your outfit and your hat. Oh and there are the flowers, hymns to choose, where you're having the reception, the menu . . . and it goes on. There are the bridesmaids to sort out, pageboys maybe, that dubious friend the best man and, of course, at the centre of it all the most important people, the happy couple – the bride and groom. Yes, everyone has to be ready for the Big Day.

In the times when Jesus told this story wedding customs were a bit different. It could all last several days, for a start, and it wasn't until the last day that the bridegroom would come for his bride. She wouldn't know the exact time or day even when he would come so she would have to wait and be ready all the time.

She had bridesmaids with her – this bride in the story had fourteen! Each bridesmaid had a little oil lamp to light the pathway of the bridegroom's procession. Because they didn't know when he would come they kept their lamps lit in readiness. They had to make sure they had enough oil to last. The lamps didn't hold much so they had to have some extra so that they could fill them up when they ran out.

Well, seven bridesmaids were sensible and had brought extra oil with them. But I'm afraid seven bridesmaids were silly and never thought about it. They only had the oil that was in their lamps. This particular bridegroom was very late coming. They were waiting and waiting.

Night time came. The girls got sleepy and nodded off. Suddenly one of them woke – 'Listen!' she cried. 'Wake up! I can hear music. He's coming.'

Quickly the girls stood up and lit their lamps which by then had gone out. The seven sensible girls filled theirs up with the extra oil they had brought. But the other seven girls were all in a panic. Oh no! No oil!

'Lend us some of yours,' they begged the other girls.

'Sorry, we only brought enough for our own lamps. If you hurry you could go and buy some and maybe you'll be back in time.'

So the girls rushed off to find somewhere to buy some oil. It took them a long time. They lit their lamps and hurried back to the Wedding Feast.

But – oh dear – whilst they had been gone the bridegroom had arrived. All the guests had gone inside. The feast had begun.

The doors were closed.

The girls could hear the music, the laughter and singing. They knocked loudly on the door. 'Open the door! Let us in! Why didn't you wait?'

At last a voice from inside said, 'Who are you? Everyone is here. We don't know of anyone else coming.'

And the door remained shut fast.

The people listening to Jesus telling the story laughed and shook their heads. 'Silly girls,' they said, 'they should have been ready.' 'But are you ready?' said Jesus, 'Are you ready for God's kingdom here on earth?'

Are we ready? This is what Jesus is saying we must be ready for – that day when he will come again. We don't know when it will be. We don't know the day or the month or the year – whether it will be morning or night. But Jesus wants us to be ready for him.

Some of the girls did keep their lights shining for the bridegroom. Jesus is sometimes called a bridegroom and the Church – that's us – is his bride. So we must be ready and keep our lights shining for his coming, whenever that may be.

Jesus will come – whether we are ready or not.

Song This little light of mine *or* Jesus bids us shine

Prayers

'No one knows about that day or hour, not even the angels in heaven, nor the Son, but only the Father . . . Therefore keep watch because you do not know what day your Lord will come.'

Today, as we prepare for the coming of Jesus, we have lit our first Advent candle. Jesus is the Light of the World, coming into the darkness and the shadows. We pray now for his light to fill our world, our lives and our hearts.

Voice one

Lord of light and love,
shine in the shadows of this dark world.
Where there is war and hatred;
where there is pain and suffering;
where there is hunger and need;
bring comfort and healing in the circle of your light.

All three voices

Jesus, Light of the World,
light up our world today.

Voice two

Lord of light and love,
shine in the shadows of our dark lives.
To those who feel lost and alone;
to those who feel despair;
to those who feel shame or guilt;
bring hope in the circle of your light.

All three voices

Jesus, Light of the World,
light up our lives today.

Voice three

Lord of light and love,
shine in the shadows of our hearts.
Open our stubborn minds to your will;

take away selfishness and pride;
fill us with the warmth of your light.

All three voices

Jesus, Light of the World,
light up our hearts today.

May we be ready and prepared for the coming of Jesus, the Light of the World, both this Christmas time and also on that glorious day when he will come as our reigning King.

The special prayer for Advent Sunday:

Almighty God,
give us grace to cast away the works of darkness
and to put on the armour of light,
now in the time of this mortal life,
in which your Son Jesus Christ came to us in great humility;
that on the last day,
when he shall come again in his glorious majesty
to judge the living and the dead,
we may rise to the life immortal;
through him who is alive and reigns with you,
in the unity of the Holy Spirit,
one God, now and for ever. Amen.

Common Worship

We say the prayer that Jesus taught us.
Our Father . . .

Statement of faith

Please stand.

We say together in faith:
holy, holy, holy
is the Lord God almighty,
who was and is and is to come.

We believe in God the Father,
who created all things:
for by his will they were created
and have their being.

We believe in God the Son,
who was slain:
for with his blood
he purchased us for God,
from every tribe and language,
from every people and nation.

We believe in God the Holy Spirit:
the Spirit and the Bride say, 'Come!'
Even so come, Lord Jesus!
Amen.

New Patterns for Worship

Song

Lord, the light of your love is shining (Shine, Jesus, shine)

Blessing

May the bright light of Christ enlighten our hearts,
shine in our minds and direct our journeying,
and give light to the world.
Maranatha! Come, Lord Jesus.

David Adam

And the blessing of God almighty, the Father, the Son, and the Holy Spirit, be among you and remain with you always. Amen.

Advent two

Colours

Have ready:

- a box with some green, red and silver decorations
- another small box with a few blue decorations
- some Christmas cards with pictures of robins and Father Christmas on them
- a poinsettia plant
- a small Christmas tree or branch
- a table with an attractive bowl and a candle
- small pieces of card or paper and pencils in the pews
- a CD of blues music from which to play a short extract *(optional)*

Choose two readers and two or three people to lead the prayers.

Welcome Good morning everybody and welcome to this service on the second Sunday in Advent. Today we can light two candles on our Advent wreath. (*Choose two people to come out and light the candles.)*

I'm sure that many of you are beginning to get more excited about Christmas as the time gets nearer. Maybe you have your decorations up already and have begun to send out your Christmas cards.

Let us not lose sight of who it is we welcome and celebrate. Let us remember our loving Saviour, who came at Christmas and who will come again.

We stand together and worship as we sing.

Song Hark, the glad sound! the Saviour comes *or* Lord, I come before your throne of grace.

Prayer This is the day the Lord has made. We will rejoice and be glad in it. Lord God, we come here today to offer our worship and our praise. Open our hearts and our minds to your word.

Confession As we come before our Lord at this particularly busy time of year, we think of the times we have failed him this week. When the Lord comes he will bring to light the things now hidden in darkness, and will disclose the purposes of our heart. Therefore in the light of Christ let us confess our sins.

God of mercy, we acknowledge that we are all sinners.
We turn from the wrong
that we have thought and said and done,
and are mindful of all that we have failed to do.
For the sake of Jesus who died for us,
forgive us all that is past
and help us to live each day
in the light of Christ our Lord.
Amen.

New Patterns for Worship

Absolution May almighty God have mercy on us,
forgive us our sins,
and bring us to everlasting life,
through Jesus Christ our Lord.
Amen.

New Patterns for Worship

Activity Christmas is a very colourful time. What colours make you think about Christmas?

(Take suggestions. Green – the Christmas tree, holly and ivy. Red – Father Christmas's coat, robins on Christmas cards, decorations on the tree, candles. Silver and gold – the star, one of the gifts the Wise Men brought, tinsel.)

Some of you children may like to come and have a look in my mystery Christmas box here and see what you can find in those lovely Christmas colours.

(Children come out and hold the objects up as they take them out of the box.)

We have some beautiful things here. We'll hang the decorations on this tree *(branch)* and stand the cards on the table for everyone to enjoy.

And look – behind the box is something else that's red. *(Hold up the poinsettia.)* We see a lot of these flowers at Christmas. Their star shape reminds us of the star of Bethlehem. Let's put it on the table with the cards. A lovely colourful Christmas.

In a moment we're going to think about another colour that we haven't got here, but before we do we'll stand and sing a song with some colours in it.

Song Colours of day (Light up the fire) *or* The holly and the ivy

Readings Now we are going to hear two readings from the Bible. One is from the Old Testament and one from the New.

Reader one

But now, this is what the Lord says –
he who created you O Jacob,
he who formed you O Israel.
'Fear not, for I have redeemed you,
I have summoned you by name; you are mine.
When you pass through the waters, I will be with you,
and when you pass through the rivers
they will not sweep over you.
When you walk through the fire, you will not be burned;
the flames will not set you ablaze.

For I am the Lord your God,
the Holy One of Israel, your Saviour . . .
Do not be afraid, for I am with you.'

Isaiah 43:1-3a, 5a (NIV)

Reader two

Then I saw a new heaven and a new earth, for the first heaven and the first earth had passed away, and there was no longer any sea. I saw the Holy City, the new Jerusalem, coming down out of heaven from God, prepared as a bride beautifully dressed for her husband. And I heard a loud voice from the throne saying, 'Now the dwelling of God is with men, and he will live with them and be their God. He will wipe away every tear from their eyes. There will be no more mourning or crying or pain, for the old order has passed away.' He who was seated on the throne said, 'I am making everything new!' Then he said, 'Write this down, for these words are trustworthy and true.'

Revelation 21:1-5 (NIV)

Talk You may have been wondering what those readings had to do with colours or Christmas. They didn't mention anything red or green, or silver or gold. They seemed to talk more about being afraid or being upset. What has that got to do with Christmas?

Back to colours – and I'm thinking about a different colour now. I'm thinking about the colour blue. I don't know about you but it's not a colour I particularly think of at Christmas. I haven't any blue decorations, or blue candles. There won't be blue icing on my Christmas cake. Snowmen aren't blue. Father Christmas doesn't wear a blue coat. The star definitely wasn't blue.

The only thing I can think of that might be blue is Mary's dress in the pictures we see on cards. We don't even know if she really did wear blue although a very pale blue was the colour that women wore in Nazareth.

I'm thinking of a different sort of blue – and it's more a feeling than a colour. It's a sad sort of blue. Sometimes if you're feeling a bit down you might say, 'I'm feeling blue today' or, 'I've got the blues'.

Some of us are old enough to remember a song called 'I never felt more like singing the blues' *(sing a bit if you like!).* Of course there is a whole style of music called the blues. It's really a sad-sounding form of jazz music.

(Optional) Listen to this short piece of blues music. *(Play an extract of blues from a CD, or if you are lucky enough to have live musicians let them play a short piece.)* Did that make you feel a bit sad?

Most blues songs are sad and usually about losing someone you love. I think there may be some people who are feeling sad and blue this Christmas because they have lost someone they love. They won't feel like joining in all the fun and celebrations. There are others too who may be lonely, hungry, poor, ill or unhappy in this country and all over the world who will find it hard to say 'Happy Christmas'.

Today we are going to think about and pray for those who have lost someone they love. Now they are facing a Christmas for the first time without that person:

- a husband without his wife
- a wife without her husband
- an adult whose mother or father has died
- young children who have lost a parent
- people who have lost their partner or another close relative or friend

We can think of families of soldiers who have been killed this year in *(place of war).* You may know someone here today who has lost somebody close to them recently. It may be the person sitting next to you, or behind you or in front of you.

There may be people here who are feeling empty inside. This is not an easy time, but as Christians we know that there is comfort to be found in the message of Christmas.

In the pews there are some cards and pencils. If you know someone who is hurting at this time – here or somewhere else, or indeed if you yourself are hurting, write a name down. In the next song come and put the card in this bowl at the front. I'm going to light this candle by the side of the names.

We'll remain seated to sing.

(The talk continues after the song.)

Song Be still, for the presence of the Lord *or* Beauty for brokenness *or* Faithful One

Talk God knows each one of us by name. He knows all these people whose names we have written down and he loves each and every one. In our readings we heard words of comfort. 'Do not be afraid, for I am with you.' 'He will wipe every tear from their eyes. There will be no more death, or mourning or crying or pain.'

God is telling us that we are not alone. He is with us. Advent reminds us that God sent his Son to come into our world to show his great love for us all. As we come to know Jesus we find that he too went through pain and suffering and so he understands the pain and suffering that people go through in any place and in any time. He understands because he has been there in those dark places himself. Think of some of the things he went through:

(You could do this part in a question-and-answer form – 'Can you think of a time when Jesus was homeless? . . . When was he a refugee?' etc.)

- He was homeless – his parents couldn't find anywhere to stay when he was born. They had to shelter in a stable.
- He was a refugee – his parents fled to another country where they would be safe from persecution and danger.
- He was hungry and met temptation in a desert.
- He was rejected by some of his family and friends.
- He wept when a dear friend died.
- He was betrayed by someone who had been a friend, then deserted and left alone.
- He was treated cruelly for a crime he didn't commit.
- He was killed on a cross.

Yet all these things were not the end. Jesus overcame them on that cross. He came to life again and is alive today and through him we can live too. We can hold on to that knowledge of his life-giving love this Christmas even if we are lonely or feel empty. The love of Jesus can fill that emptiness. 'Do not be afraid. I am with you.'

We can smile at Christmas in the light of his love. We can look through the door into the stable and smile. We can hear the songs the angels sing and smile.

Now, in this box I have a few more decorations for our tree *(branch)*. And yes, these decorations are blue. We'll hang them among all the other colours. The silver and gold will shine on the blue and make it sparkle. *(Hand the decorations out to some children for them to hang up.)*

That looks lovely. Now let us pray.

Prayers

Let us be quiet for a moment and think of those we know, as well as those we do not know, who will be facing Christmas alone this year and who will find it hard to join in the fun and excitement. If you wrote someone's name on a card, think about that person now. Let us pray that Christmas will be a time of healing; a time of light, love and renewal.

Voice one

When the lights of the city are bright but cold;
when careless friends rush by;
when wealth and pleasure fade with the dying day;
O Lord, bring comfort in a healing time.

Voice two

When lonely voices cry at night;
when all seems empty and lost:
when days ahead look dark and skies are grey;
O Lord, bring comfort in a healing time.

Voice three

In love there is no fear at all;
Jesus knows each name;
even in the darkest night he is very near,
O Lord bring comfort in a healing time.

We pray that in these noisy, fun-filled days we may see the face of Jesus and follow him in his way.

Lord Jesus,
show us the path to the stable
and the road to the cross.
In a self-seeking, pleasure-seeking world
direct us in your way.
Turn our faces to your face;
our eyes to your sacrifice;
our minds to your will;
and our hearts to your love.
In your name we pray.
Amen.

The special prayer for the second Sunday in Advent:

O Lord raise up, we pray, your power
and come among us,
and with your great might succour us;
that whereas, through our sins and wickedness
we are grievously hindered
in running the race that is set before us,
your bountiful grace and mercy
may speedily help and deliver us;
through Jesus Christ, your Son our Lord,
to whom with you and the Holy Spirit,
be honour and glory, now and for ever.
Amen.

Common Worship

We say together the prayer Jesus taught us.
Our Father . . .

Statement of faith

And now we stand to declare what we believe.

Do you believe and trust in God the Father,
source of being and life,
the one for whom we exist?
We believe and trust in him.

Do you believe and trust in God the Son,
who took our human nature,
died for us and rose again?
We believe and trust in him.

Do you believe and trust in God the Holy Spirit,
who gives life to the people of God
and makes Christ known in the world?
We believe and trust in him.

This is the faith of the Church.
This is our faith.
We believe and trust in one God,
Father, Son and Holy Spirit.
Amen.

Common Worship

And so we join together to sing a great hymn of assurance in the knowledge of God's love and faithfulness.

Song Great is thy faithfulness

Blessing Grace, mercy and peace from God the Father and from Jesus Christ, the Father's Son, will be with us in truth and love.

2 John 1:3 (NIV)

And the blessing of God almighty, the Father, the Son, and the Holy Spirit, be among you and remain with you always. Amen.

Go in peace to love and serve the Lord.
In the name of Christ, amen.

Advent three

Messengers and messages

The leader needs to have a mobile phone and someone in the congregation primed to send a text message and to make a call.
Also required:

- a postman with four large envelopes with messages in
- four young people to open the envelopes and read the messages
- John the Baptist to be interviewed by the leader. He should be dressed in rough clothes if possible

Have scripts prepared for the leader and John the Baptist.

Welcome Welcome to our service on this the third Sunday in Advent. We have three candles to light today on our Advent wreath. *(Choose children to come and light the candles.)*

Today we are going to think about people who prepared the way for the coming of Jesus. So we stand to sing.

Song O come, O come Emmanuel *or* Make way, make way

As we make way for the coming of the Lord let us make way for him in our hearts as well. We acknowledge that we often fail him and fall short of what he wants us to be. We bring these failings to him now and ask his forgiveness.

Confession **Most merciful God,**
Father of our Lord Jesus Christ,
we confess that we have sinned
in thought, word and deed.
We have not loved you with our whole heart.
We have not loved our neighbours as ourselves.
In your mercy
forgive what we have been,

help us to amend what we are,
and direct what we shall be;
that we may do justly,
love mercy,
and walk humbly with you, our God.
Amen.

Common Worship

Absolution

Almighty God,
who forgives all who truly repent,
have mercy upon *you,*
pardon and deliver *you* from all your sins,
confirm and strengthen *you* in all goodness,
and keep you in life eternal;
through Jesus Christ our Lord.
Amen.

Common Worship

Activity

(Make sure you have your mobile phone in your pocket and a friend primed!)

In a few moments we are going to hear some words from the Bible. These will tell– *(mobile phone rings).* Oh no! I'm so sorry everyone. I thought I'd turned it off. *(Look at phone.)* It says I've got two missed calls as well. Now why is she phoning me? She knows I'm busy this morning. *(Answer phone.)* I'm sorry I can't talk now. I'm in the middle of something. Bye.

I do apologise. Now, where was I? Oh yes, I was going to tell you about our readings from the Bible today. In the book of– *(phone bleeps with a text message).* I don't believe this. *(Look at phone.)* What does he want? Oh, I can't read it now.

I'll start again! A long time ago there were prophets who– *(another text message comes through).* This is getting ridiculous. I am going to turn it off now. There. Hopefully there won't be any more interruptions.

I'm beginning to get confused. All this has quite put me off. So many messages – I wonder if they were important? But to get back to what I was saying: here we are, well into Advent, thinking about the coming of Jesus, preparing for Christmas, singing our Advent hymns and songs and–

(Loud voice from the back of the church)

Postman: Post! Special delivery here for the people of *(name your church or town).* Who's in charge here? *(Walks to the front.)*

Leader: Well, I suppose I am.

(Postman hands over four large envelopes.)

Postman: Sign here please.

Leader: Here? They must be important if I have to sign for them. Thank you.

(Exit postman.)

(Look at the addresses.) Someone really is trying to get in touch with us today. These are all addressed to 'The Church of *(name of church)* in *(name of town)*'. First I have phone calls and then text messages. Now it's the post. I wouldn't be surprised if there's a load of emails waiting for me when I get home as well. Would some of you come and help me with these letters? Let's open this one and see what it says. Could you read it out to everyone please?

Reader one: *(Opens first letter.)*
Dear people of *(name of your church),*
Arise, shine, for your light has come,
and the glory of the Lord rises upon you.
See, darkness covers the earth
and thick darkness is over the peoples,
but the Lord rises upon you
and his glory appears before you.

Nations will come to your light,
and kings to the brightness of your dawn.
Lift up your eyes and look about you.
Yours sincerely,
Isaiah

Isaiah 60:1-4a (NIV)

Leader: Isaiah. I've heard of him. That sounds as if he is giving us a wake-up call. Let's hear what the second letter has to say.

Reader two: *(Opens second letter.)*
Dear friends,
The people walking in darkness have seen a great light;
on those living in the land of the shadow of death
a light has dawned.
For to us a child is born, to us a son is given,
and the government will be upon his shoulders.
And he will be called
Wonderful Counsellor, Mighty God,
Everlasting Father, Prince of Peace.
Of the increase of his government and peace
there will be no end.
He will reign on David's throne and over his kingdom,
establishing and upholding it with justice and righteousness
from that time on and for ever.
The zeal of the Lord Almighty will accomplish this.
With all good wishes from
Isaiah

Isaiah 9:2, 6, 7 (NIV)

Leader: It's from Isaiah again. He's very keen to get his message across – more about light in darkness and then the coming of a child. There are still two more letters to open. I wonder who this one is from. Let's look.

Reader three: *(Opens third letter.)*
It's from someone called Micah.
Dear people of *(name),*
Hear, O peoples, all of you.
Listen, O earth and all who are in it,
that the Sovereign Lord may witness against you,
the Lord from his holy temple.
Look! The Lord is coming from his dwelling place;
he comes down and treads the places of the earth.
But you, Bethlehem Ephrathah,
though you are little among the clans of Judah,
out of you will come for me one who will rule over Israel.
Yours faithfully,
Micah

Micah 1:2, 3; 5:2 (NIV)

Leader: I think we're beginning to get the message here. Micah is telling us the place where all this will happen. We'll open the last letter. Who's this one from?

Reader four: *(Opens the fourth letter.)*
It's from Isaiah again. It's very short. He says:
Dear friends,
Therefore the Lord himself will give you a sign:
The virgin will be with child
and will give birth to a son,
and will call him Immanuel.
Yours sincerely,
Isaiah

Isaiah 7:14 (NIV)

Leader: I think we're getting the message loud and clear from Isaiah and from Micah – all those wake-up words! 'Arise', 'see', 'look', 'hear', 'listen'. What are they telling us? A light is coming to shine in this dark world. This light is from God. There will be a birth of someone incredibly important and wonderful. We are even told where this will happen – in Bethlehem. There was someone else as well who prepared the way for the coming of Jesus – another messenger, John the Baptist. Before we hear more about him we'll sing again.

Song On Jordan's bank the Baptist's cry *or* From the distant east and the farthest west (The Preparation)

Talk As we have heard, the prophets foretold the coming of the Messiah. Isaiah spoke clearly of what and who was to come. He also spoke about someone else. 'I will send my messenger ahead of you, who will prepare your way, a voice of one calling in the desert–

(Loud voice from the back of the church. Enter John the Baptist. He walks down the church speaking loudly.)

John: Prepare the way of the Lord, make straight paths for him. Repent, for the kingdom of heaven is at hand!

Leader: I think we know who this is. Welcome – it's John the Baptist isn't it?

John: That is what they call me.

Leader: Will you answer a few questions for us this morning?

John: I will answer what I can.

Leader: Thank you. First, please tell us why you are here and the message you have for us.

John: My message is simple. Repent – turn from your old ways, be baptised and washed clean. Your sins will be forgiven.

Leader: Is it really as straightforward as that?

John: Couldn't be simpler.

Leader: I understand you lead a simple life too. Your clothes are rough I see. What are they made of? Is it camel's hair, and all held together with a belt of leather?

John: Yes, that's right. My clothes aren't important though.

Leader: I heard that you live out in the desert and have a – well, an unusual diet. Is that correct?

John: My needs are few. I want to concentrate on the job I have been given so I don't waste time with fancy food or a luxurious home. Locusts and wild honey do me nicely and a blanket under the stars at night is enough.

Leader: Hmm – interesting . . . Have you travelled far in your work?

John: I've been in the whole region around Jordan proclaiming my message.

Leader: Is it true that many crowds have gathered to listen to you? And do I also hear that you are – well, outspoken to say the least? You call a spade a spade?

John: Yes, many people have come to hear what I have to say and they need to hear the truth. I believe I may have called them snakes at one time, which I admit is quite strong. But I want to tell people how great and powerful God is and how, in comparison, they have all have done much to be ashamed of. I tell them how they should lead good lives – lives that are worthy and fruitful. I remind them that they need to repent and ask forgiveness for their wrongdoing in the past.

Leader: 'Repent' – that's a strong word too. Doesn't it mean 'be really sorry'; 'turn from your old ways'?

John: That's right – I want people to admit that they are doing wrong, to stop in their tracks, turn around and go a different way, God's way. Oh, often they don't understand! 'What shall we do?' they say.

Leader: So what do you tell them?

John: Share your possessions with those who have none. Give food to those who are hungry. I tell tax collectors to take only what is required and no more. I tell soldiers to be satisfied with their wages and not try to get money from people with threats and lies.

Leader: And so you baptise people as an outward sign of this change in their lives – as if they are being washed clean?

John: Yes indeed, but my message, my baptism is nothing compared to what, and who, is to come.

Leader: Can you explain that?

John: I'm afraid some of the people who have listened to me think I am the Messiah – the Promised One – but I am not I can assure you. No, there is one coming after me who is much greater, much more powerful, than I am. I am not fit to tie his shoes. I baptise with water – that's all it is. The one who is coming will baptise with the Holy Spirit.

Leader: Well thank you John for coming here and talking to us this morning. We're very grateful.

(John leaves, going down the church again shouting, 'Repent! The kingdom of heaven is at hand. Prepare the way of the Lord. Repent!' as he exits.)

The powerful message from John the Baptist – and this is how the Bible tells us how his words came true.

Reader one

The next day he saw Jesus coming toward him and declared, 'Here is the Lamb of God who takes away the sin of the world!' This is he of whom I said, 'After me comes a man who ranks ahead of me because he was before me. I myself did not know him but I came baptising with water for this reason that he might be revealed to Israel.'

And John testified, 'I saw the Spirit descending from heaven like a dove and it remained on him. I myself did not know him but the one who sent me to baptise with water said to me, "He on whom you see the Spirit descend and remain is the one who baptises with the Holy Spirit."

And I myself have seen and testified that this is the Son of God.'

John 1:29-34 (NRSV)

John recognised Jesus for who he was – the Son of God. We live in a world where we are constantly bombarded with information, with news, with messages. The mobile phone has become a 'must-have' part of our lives. We are all instantly accessible. We sit at our computers and go to our inbox for our messages – 'You've got mail'. We share personal news on Facebook and opinions on Twitter. On the internet, news flashes round the world in an instant. But as fast as it appears it just as quickly disappears when something different, something more shocking, more 'newsworthy', takes place. A dramatic, tragic or scandalous event takes over our television screens for a week and then it's on to something else and we forget all about it.

God's messages are so different! God's messages are eternal. They are not just this week's news to be pushed aside by something else next week. Isaiah, Micah, Jeremiah, the writers of the psalms and, of course, John the Baptist all had messages to tell us about the coming Messiah – real, living messages.

God's word in the Bible is for all time. It's not here today and gone tomorrow. The messengers of Advent prepared the way for the coming of Jesus as the one who came down to earth as a man and who will come again as a King.

Are we listening? Do we hear these messages? Let's listen. Let's hear. And let us be prepared in our hearts and in our lives for Jesus to enter in as our Lord and Saviour.

Song The light of Christ *or* Purify my heart

Prayers Let us pray.

Blessed are you, Lord our God,
for you sent your messengers and prophets
to tell of your coming.
As John the Baptist was a burning and shining light
in the darkness,
help us to show your presence in our daily life.

David Adam

The special prayer for the third Sunday in Advent:

O Lord Jesus Christ,
who at your first coming sent your messenger
to prepare your way before you;
grant that the ministers and stewards of your mysteries
may likewise so prepare and make ready your way
by turning the hearts of the disobedient
to the wisdom of the just,
that at your second coming to judge the world
we may be found an acceptable people in your sight;
for you are alive and reign with the Father
in the unity of the Holy Spirit,
our God, now and for ever.

Common Worship

We bring before God those places in the world where there is trouble and discord.

We pray for . . .

We think of our own country at this time; for our leaders, that they will govern with wisdom and integrity.

We pray for . . .

We pray for the Church of God both far and near; for fellow Christians all over the world, especially those who are persecuted for their faith.

We pray for . . .

We pray for the work of our own church, that we may share the gospel message in our own community.

We especially pray for . . .

We pray for those who are ill in body or in spirit; for those who are in trouble or distress; those who are hungry or in need.

We especially pray for . . .

Merciful Father,
accept these prayers for the sake of your Son,
our Saviour Jesus Christ.
Amen.

We say together the Lord's Prayer.
Our Father . . .

Statement of faith

Let us stand to declare what we believe.

We say together in faith:
holy, holy, holy
is the Lord God almighty,
who was and is and is to come.

We believe in God the Father,
who created all things:
for by his will they were created
and have their being.

We believe in God the Son who was slain:
for with his blood
he purchased us for God,
from every tribe and language,
from every people and nation.

We believe in God the Holy Spirit:
the Spirit and the Bride say 'Come!'
Even so come, Lord Jesus!
Amen.

New Patterns for Worship

Song

Go forth and tell *or* You shall go out with joy

Blessing

As we go out with joy may the blessing of God almighty, the Father, the Son, and the Holy Spirit, be among you and remain with you always. Amen.

So let us go in peace to love and serve the Lord.
In the name of Christ.
Amen.

Advent four

Mary – ready and willing

Have a large photograph album ready. This is sufficient but if you wish, and have the equipment, you could prepare a selection of photographs for the talk, to show on a screen:

- a newborn baby
- a christening
- a church
- a wedding
- a cross
- a garden and an empty tomb (If possible! A beautiful garden filled with sunlight would do.)

Prepare four large pieces of card with the letters M, A, R, Y written on them. On four more cards have the words 'mother', 'amazed', 'reign' and 'yes'. Ask someone to mime the part of Mary. All it involves is sitting and looking through a photograph album. Also required are four readers.

Welcome Good morning everyone and welcome to our service on the fourth Sunday in Advent – the last Sunday before Christmas. There's not long to go! How many more sleeps, children? We can light four candles on our Advent wreath today. *(Choose some children to come out and light the candles.)* Just one candle left now, there in the middle, to light on Christmas Day.

We come to worship in praise and celebration as we look forward to the Christmas festival. So let us stand together and sing.

Song Hail to the Lord's anointed *or* Come on and celebrate

Let us sit or kneel and be quiet for a few moments. Think back over the week that has passed. There will have been times when we haven't got things quite right. Maybe we've said something unkind or untruthful. Maybe we have hurt somebody. Perhaps we have failed to do something we should have done. In these busy days before Christmas it's easy to get so caught up in all that we have to do that we forget what is more important.

Whatever we have got wrong this week let us bring it to God our Father now, and ask him to forgive us as we say together–

Confession

Father, we have sinned against heaven and against you.
We are not worthy to be called your children.
We turn to you again.
Have mercy on us,
bring us back to yourself
as those who once were dead
but now have life through Christ our Lord.
Amen.

New Patterns for Worship

Absolution

May the God of love
bring *us* back to himself,
forgive *us our* sins,
and assure *us* of his eternal love
in Jesus Christ our Lord.
Amen.

New Patterns for Worship

Activity

Today we think about someone who plays a very important part in the Christmas story. If I say, 'You may know *her* name,' that gives a clue. Who is it? Yes, it's Mary.

Here are the letters that spell her name. First of all, 'M' *(show card)*. Will someone come out and hold this up for me? The first thing that Mary was told was that she was going to be a mother. Listen to what it says in St Luke's Gospel.

Reader one

In the sixth month, God sent the angel Gabriel to Nazareth, a town in Galilee, to a virgin pledged to be married to a man named Joseph, a descendant of David. The virgin's name was Mary. The angel went to her and said, 'Greetings, you who are highly favoured! The Lord is with you.'

Mary was greatly troubled at his words and wondered what kind of greeting this might be. But the angel said to her, 'Do not be afraid, Mary, you have found favour with God. You will be with child and give birth to a son, and you are to give him the name Jesus.

Luke 1:26-31 (NIV)

Mary was told she would be a **mother**. *(Show card with the word 'mother' written on it.)* Will someone come and hold this card up for me? She was going to be a mother. I think Mary would have been surprised to say the least – and maybe a bit frightened. Listen to what Luke tells us next.

Reader two

He will be great and will be called the Son of the Most High. The Lord God will give him the throne of his father David, and he will reign over the house of Jacob for ever; his kingdom will never end. 'How will this be,' Mary asked the angel, 'since I am a virgin?'

Luke 1:32-34 (NIV)

Mary was shocked, surprised and probably frightened. She was **amazed**. *(Hold up card with the word 'amazed' written on it.)* Will someone come and hold this for me? She didn't understand. The angel explained to her.

Reader three

The angel answered, 'The Holy Spirit will come upon you, and the power of the Most High will overshadow you. So the holy one to be born will be called the Son of God.

Luke 1:35 (NIV)

I can think of a few words beginning with 'r'. Mary **realised** that her son was going to be a Very Important Person. He would be the Son of God and also a King – a King who would **reign** over all. We'll have the word 'reign' to hold up and that will remind us that Jesus will be a King. We need someone else out here to hold it. And there are two more words beginning with 'r'. How did Mary **respond**? What was her **reply**? Listen again.

Reader four

'I am the Lord's servant,' Mary answered. 'May it be to me as you have said.' Then the angel left her.

Luke 1:38 (NIV)

Mary didn't say, 'Why?' She didn't say, 'What, me?' She didn't say, 'I'd really rather not, thank you.' She heard what the angel said. She listened to everything. She knew he was from God and she was ready to obey. She accepted and said she was God's servant and would do his will.

Mary said 'Yes**'.** So that's our last word. *(Hold up the word 'yes'.)* Will someone come and hold this for me? Mary – a **mother** who heard the message and was **amazed**. She would have a son who would be a King and **reign** over everyone. She said '**yes**' to God. I wonder if we listen to what God has to say to us. What is our response?

Song Jesus, take me as I am *or* I will offer up my life

Talk Let's get to know some more about Mary because I think she was a rather amazing person. Look – here she comes.

(Enter Mary. She is holding a large photograph album. She sits on a chair in a place where she can be seen by everyone.)

What's she carrying? Oh, it's a photograph album. Well, I know they didn't have photograph albums then, but let's imagine they did. Mary is looking back and remembering.

I love looking at photographs. These days of course we can store them on our computer and we probably take hundreds with our digital cameras. I don't know about you but I still like to have prints made. I like to carry some around so that I can show people *(name people you like to show pictures of, e.g. children/grandchildren/family)* and I like to browse through old albums with all the memories that they conjure up – the holidays, the family occasions, those annual school photographs, Sports Days, that Cup match!

So we'll imagine Mary having a family photograph album. I wonder what pictures she would have kept in it? *(Mary begins to look through the album. Leader goes to look over her shoulder.)* Ah, I guessed as much – a newborn baby. *(If you wish, put up pictures on a screen or have some of your own to hold up.)* She would certainly have a picture of the baby Jesus – lots, probably.

Now who's this – someone else standing with Mary? It's another mother – they've both got baby boys. I know who it is – it's her cousin Elizabeth. She was rather special too and, like Mary, she and her husband were told by an angel that they would have a baby boy even though Elizabeth was quite old. Her son was called John, who we know as John the Baptist. Mary went to see her after the Angel Gabriel had been.

Next picture. It looks like a christening. Someone – looks like the vicar – is holding the baby Jesus. Anyone know who he might be? His name was Simeon, a devout man who waited and longed for the Messiah. Mary and Joseph have taken the baby to the temple as the law at the time said they must.

Now what's Mary looking at? It's a family group. Mary and Joseph and several children; Jesus is the tallest. He's the eldest. I think the most photographs I have are of holidays. Pictures at the seaside, picnics, swimming, making sandcastles, eating ice cream. I wonder if Mary and Joseph ever went on holiday with their children?

What's this picture? It's Mary and Joseph, children – that one must be Jesus – and quite a crowd of others too. They are at the temple in Jerusalem. They went there every year with lots of people. It was a holiday and a time of celebration. Jesus looks about twelve in the photograph. They were away for a few days but on the way home Mary and Joseph lost Jesus. They were so worried. They found him in the end though, sitting talking with teachers and priests. I don't think Mary was too pleased at the time but later on she came to understand more about the work that Jesus had to do.

Oh, here's a nice picture. It's a wedding. I can see Jesus. It's quite a few years later. He's a man now. There's Mary and they're with lots of friends. I know what Mary will be remembering. It will be the time they were all guests at a wedding where there was nearly a disaster. They ran out of wine. The hosts were in a panic, I can tell you. But Mary – see, she's smiling – knew by then just how special Jesus was. She told the servants, the waiters, to do what Jesus told them to do. Jesus told them to fill the empty jars with water. To their amazement when they lifted the jars to pour, the water had become wine! Mary was very proud of her son that day. *(Mary turns the pages – sometimes smiling, sometimes shaking her head.)*

She's coming to the end of the album. There aren't many more pictures. But now she seems to look sad. I wonder what she's looking at. *(Look over her shoulder.)* It's a picture of a cross. I'm sure she must remember that day more than any other. In the Bible we read that Mary stood at the foot of the cross when Jesus was crucified. That must have been the hardest thing for a mother to do – to watch her son die.

But she hasn't come to the end of the album yet. That wasn't the last picture. What's next? Ah – it's a picture of a garden and an empty tomb. Mary looks happier now.

(Mary walks away.)

I don't expect Mary had any idea what the future held for her and her son when she said 'yes' to the angel all that time ago, when she was only a teenager. It was a long, hard road for her to travel – the road that led all the way from that bleak little stable to a cross on a lonely hill. I expect along the way she laughed and cried. I expect she was both proud of her son and puzzled by him and I'm sure that she suffered great pain and distress as she watched the path he had to take. There would have been much that she didn't understand for a long time. But eventually she would have known joy when she, with the others, saw him alive again, just as we can today.

Mary said 'Yes' to God – as we can. She put her trust in God – as we can. She followed Jesus – as we can.

Song From heaven you came (The Servant King)

Prayers Let us pray.

Mary heard the angel and wondered at his words;
she bowed her head and accepted God's will.
Like Mary, may we hear his words to us;
know the truth of his promises;
and as Mary did, give our hearts and our lives to him.

Mary was a mother. She had a family.
We pray for families today.
We pray that parents will teach their children wisely;
that children will learn what is right and what is wrong.
We pray for families where there is hardship –
illness, sadness, poverty, brokenness –
and we ask for God's comfort and healing.

At this time of Christmas, this family time,
may we share together God's rich blessing
in the birth of his Son.

The special prayer for the fourth Sunday in Advent:

God our redeemer,
who prepared the Blessed Virgin Mary
to be the mother of your Son;
grant that, as she looked for his coming as our saviour,
so we may be ready to greet him
when he comes again as our judge;
who is alive and reigns with you,
in the unity of the Holy Spirit,
one God, now and for ever.

Common Worship

We say together the Lord's Prayer.
Our Father . . .

Statement of faith

We stand to declare what we believe.

**We believe in God the Father,
from whom every family
in heaven and on earth is named.**

**We believe in God the Son,
who lives in our hearts through faith,
and fills us with his love.**

**We believe in God the Holy Spirit,
who strengthens us
with power from on high.**

**We believe in Father, Son and Holy Spirit.
Amen.**

Common Worship

We stand to sing our final song – Mary's great hymn of praise.

Song Tell out my soul

Blessing May God himself, the God of peace,
make you perfect and holy,
and keep you all safe and blameless,
in spirit, soul and body,
for the coming of our Lord Jesus Christ.
New Patterns for Worship

And the blessing of God almighty, the Father, the Son, and the Holy Spirit, be among you and remain with you always. Amen.

Christmas Eve

Telling the story

For this simple dramatisation of the Christmas story you need to cajole, coax and encourage the adults in your congregation to take part! A small amount of rehearsal will be necessary.

If you have a music group they could perhaps prepare one or two items in addition to the usual congregational carols. Suggestions are included for carols and songs which are all familiar. You may prefer your own choices, as appropriate for your church and congregation.

Characters

- Isaiah
- Luke
- Matthew
- Angel Gabriel
- Mary (if you have a young and willing mother with a small and obliging baby, wonderful!)
- Joseph
- Shepherds (how about using your men's group if you have one?)
- Wise Men (dare I suggest your clergy or readers?)
- King Herod and entourage of a few people
- Extras, if wanted, for the crowd in Bethlehem and Herod's entourage

Isaiah, Luke and Matthew are the main narrators, so good, clear speakers are wanted for these parts! They have the most to say so can have written scripts. Other parts have just a few words that it would be good to have learnt by heart.

Scenery is optional, minimum being a manger, maximum as much as any creative folk in your church want to do! But do have your characters dressed up appropriately.

If you have the equipment, use powerpoint or an overhead projector for the words to all the carols. Otherwise use a carol sheet and give out an order of service with a list of the numbers. Bible quotations throughout the dramatisation are taken from the NIV.

Welcome Welcome to our church on this Christmas Eve. If you are visiting us or if you are here for the very first time you are especially welcome. Today we have a story to tell you – and what a story it is! Stories don't come any better than this one!

It's great to see so many children here. Now – who has been in a nativity play at school or nursery? Did you have lots of special songs to sing and did you dress up? *(Spend a few minutes asking children and letting them say a little bit about what they have been doing.)* Well, today it's your turn to watch and listen. There will be carols and songs for you to join in with as we go along.

Before the story starts let us be quiet for a moment. *(Pause.)*

As we hear again the words of the prophets,
the songs of the angels
and the Good News of Christmas,
may our ears hear the message,
may our eyes see the star
and our voices sing in praise and thanksgiving.
May our hearts know God's love for each one of us,
through his Son, Jesus Christ, our Lord and Saviour.
Amen.

We begin by standing to sing together.

Song Once in royal David's City

Please sit.

*(**Isaiah** calls from the back of the church.)* People of *(name of your church/town/village)* I have a message for you. *(He walks down the church addressing everyone.)* My name is Isaiah and God has spoken to me and he is speaking to everyone here. Are you ready to hear his message?

I've written his words down so that I won't forget them. I'm going to read them to you now. Listen. 'The people walking in darkness have seen a great light; on those living in the land of the shadow of death a light has dawned. For to us a child is born; to us a son is given and the government shall be upon his shoulders; and he will be called Wonderful Counsellor, Mighty God, Everlasting Father, Prince of Peace.'

These are the words God gave to me. Watch and listen as you see and hear how God kept his promises.

(Isaiah moves to the side. He should remain in the choir stalls or at the clergy desk.)

(Enter ***Luke****. He goes into the pulpit or stands in a prominent place at the front.)* Hello children, parents and friends. My name is Luke and it's good to see you all here today. I want to tell you about some amazing events that happened a long time ago.

I talked to a lot of people and I decided that I must write down everything they told me, so that anyone can hear the story and remember it, because as *(name of leader)* said this is quite some story!

I want to tell you first of all about a very special person. Her name was Mary, and here she is.

(Enter ***Mary****. She can move around, working – either cleaning, sewing or baking, but occasionally stopping and dreaming a bit.)*

Now something very extraordinary and important happened to Mary. It was a bit scary for her at first but as she came to understand more she realised how amazing God's love was and what he wanted her to do. This is what happened.

There she was one day going about her usual jobs – maybe cooking, maybe cleaning, doing jobs for her mum, I don't really know. I do know that she was looking forward to getting married to Joseph. I think she may well have been dreaming about her wedding day. But then – here's the surprising bit – God sent his angel, Gabriel, to speak to her.

(Enter ***Angel Gabriel*** *and speaks to Mary)* Greetings you who are highly favoured. The Lord is with you.

Luke: 'Mary was greatly troubled at his words and wondered what kind of a greeting this might be.'

Angel Gabriel: Do not be afraid, Mary. You have found favour with God. You will be with child and give birth to a Son and you are to give him the name Jesus.

Luke: The angel went on to say that the baby would be great and called the Son of the Most High. 'The Lord God will give him the throne of his father David and he will reign over the house of Jacob for ever; his kingdom will never end.' That was quite some message! Mary was stunned at first and didn't understand it at all.

Mary: How can this be?

Luke: Mary had not yet married Joseph and she had never been with any other man. The angel explained it to her.

Angel Gabriel: The Holy Spirit will come upon you and the power of the Most High will overshadow you.

Luke: What a message for Mary to take in! But do you know? Something happened to Mary then. She understood that she had been chosen by God and she accepted it and, what's more, she even sang about it!

Mary: I am the Lord's servant. May it be to me as you have said.

(Exit Mary and Angel Gabriel.)

Song Tell out my soul *or* Come on and celebrate

(Enter ***Matthew*** *to stand on the opposite side to Luke.)*

Matthew: I think I need to take over now and fill in some more of the story. My name is Matthew and like Luke over there I talked to a lot of people and found things out that were enough to make my hair stand on end I can tell you!

You didn't get this bit did you Luke? I've talked to people who knew Joseph and I want to tell you about him. It wasn't only a shock for Mary – it was a shock for Joseph too. But you know the older I get the more I begin to understand that God has his own way of going about things and we have to accept his will because we know it's for the best.

Here he is. *(Enter **Joseph.** He walks about a bit then sits down and puts his head in his hands.)* This is Joseph and he is looking a bit worried. He's a good man and he wants to do what's right but he doesn't know what to do about Mary. Oh listen – I've written it down. This is what happened. *(Leafs through pages, running through words.)* Der-de-der de-der . . . ah yes, this is the bit, here we are.

'Mary was pledged to be married to Joseph but, before they came together, she was found to be with child through the Holy Spirit. Because Joseph, her husband, was a righteous man,' *(look round)* – that's what I told you, didn't I? A good man. Anyway, where was I? Oh yes – 'and he did not want to expose her to public disgrace, he had in mind to divorce her quietly. But after he had considered this, an angel of the Lord appeared to him in a dream.'

*(Enter **Angel Gabriel.**)*

Angel Gabriel: Joseph, son of David, do not be afraid to take Mary home as your wife, because what is conceived in her is from the Holy Spirit.

Matthew: The angel went on to say that Mary would give birth to a son and Joseph must give him the name 'Jesus' because he would save his people from their sins. And that is another of God's promises. Isaiah over there had something to say about that, didn't you my friend?

Isaiah: Indeed I did. I wrote down the very words God told me: 'Therefore the Lord himself will give you a sign: the virgin will be with child and will give birth to a son and will call him Immanuel.' Immanuel – that means, 'God with us'.

(Exit Angel Gabriel. Joseph moves to bring Mary forward.)

Song Be still, for the presence of the Lord *or* Like a candle flame *(music group only) or* The angel Gabriel from heaven came

Luke: And now I'd like to take up the story again. It was a busy time when Mary and Joseph got married. One of the first things they had to do was to obey a command from the Roman Emperor, no less. 'In those days Caesar Augustus issued a decree that a census should be taken of all the Roman world. And everyone went to their own town to register. So Joseph went up from the town of Nazareth in Galilee to Judea, to Bethlehem, the town of David because he belonged to the house and line of David.'

Matthew: *(Leafing through his papers.)* Didn't I tell you? Here it is, yes, I wrote it down – more of God's promises coming true. It wasn't you this time though was it Isaiah?

Isaiah: No – chap called Micah and I believe his words were: 'But you Bethlehem Ephrathah, though you are small among the clans of Judah, out of you will come for me one who will be ruler over Israel, whose origins are from old, from ancient times.'

Matthew: There – I knew I had got it right.

Luke: Quite so. Now let's carry on. Joseph and Mary set off to go to Bethlehem. It was quite a long way from Nazareth – a good fifty miles I reckon, so I guess they might have needed a donkey.

Song Little Donkey

(Mary and Joseph walk round the church as 'Little Donkey' is sung.)

Luke: When they got to Bethlehem it was very busy – crowds of people like Joseph and Mary, all there to register and all of them needing somewhere to stay.

(If you want you can have crowds of 'extras' milling about. Joseph and Mary can push through them – 'Excuse me, can we get through? . . . Excuse me, we're looking for a bed for the night . . . My wife needs to lie down . . .')

As you can see, Mary and Joseph are having a bit of a rough time of it. I don't know if Joseph knew anybody or had any relatives there but he couldn't find anyone who had any room for them to stay the night.

Poor Mary had nearly reached the time for the baby to be born. She wasn't looking forward to it, being in a strange place with nobody around that she knew. She so wished her mum could have been with her.

(Crowds melt away. Mary and Joseph move to the centre with their backs to the congregation, picking up the baby – real or a doll – on the way. Joseph puts his arm around Mary. As Luke reads the words they turn to the manger with the baby. Mary can hold the baby or put it in the manger.)

And yes, while they were there, 'the time came for the baby to be born and she gave birth to her firstborn, a son. She wrapped him in cloths and placed him in a manger, because there was no room for them in the inn.'

(Have a few moments of stillness and quiet.)

Song *(Remain seated.)* Silent night *or* Born in the night *(music group only)*

Luke: That wasn't all that happened that night in Bethlehem. There were some shepherds living in the fields nearby, keeping watch over their flocks at night.

(Enter shepherds from the back, talking to each other as they come – joking a bit, maybe grumbling, an older shepherd giving a young one a bit of a push. They settle down near the front and continue to talk among themselves but gradually become quiet, some nodding off to sleep. Dim the lights.)

Luke: There they were, minding their own business, a bit sleepy and quiet – it was the middle of the night, after all – when the strangest thing happened. I tell you, it was a night for strange happenings.

(Lights back on. Enter ***Angel Gabriel.****)*

'An angel of the Lord appeared to them, and the glory of the Lord shone around them and they were terrified.' Well, you would be wouldn't you? Not what you expect on an ordinary working night.

Angel Gabriel: Do not be afraid, I bring good news of great joy that will be for all people. Today in the town of David a Saviour has been born to you; he is Christ the Lord. This will be a sign to you. You will find a baby wrapped in cloths lying in a manger.

(Exit Angel Gabriel to recorded music, e.g. 'Glory to God' or a short extract from the 'Hallelujah Chorus' from Handel's Messiah.*)*

(Shepherds talk to each other, for example, 'Did you see what I just saw? . . . Was that an angel? . . . For a minute I was so scared . . . Me too. And what was all that about a Saviour? . . . Should we go? What do you think? . . . I think we should. Come on – let's see if we can find

this baby . . . Did he really say it'll be in a manger? . . . That's what I heard . . . Oh come on . . .')

Luke: 'So they hurried off and found Mary and Joseph and the baby, who was lying in a manger.'

Song While shepherds watched

(During the carol shepherds hurry round the church and back to Mary and Joseph and the baby. They look and kneel then move to the side.)

Luke: You can imagine it, can't you? Those shepherds were over the moon. They realised that they had seen something quite amazing and incredibly important. They knew it was such great news they couldn't keep it to themselves. They had to tell everyone. 'They spread the word concerning what they had been told about this child and all who heard it were amazed at what the shepherds said to them.'

(Shepherds go off in different directions round the church, talking excitedly to people in the congregation, for example, 'Do you know what we've just seen? . . . You'll never believe this! . . . A baby – in a manger! . . . There in a stable with animals . . . A Saviour – that's what the angel said . . . He's come for us all . . . That's you and me.')

Luke: 'And then they went on their way, glorifying and praising God for all the things they had heard and seen, which were just as they had been told.'

(Shepherds move away calling and shouting as they go, 'Praise the Lord! Glory be to God! Hallelujah!')

Luke: Now it's over to you again Matthew.

Matthew: Indeed, thank you Luke. Well, not only was all this excitement going on in Bethlehem but far away, in another country, there were more signs and mysteries and questions being asked.

There were these Wise Men – here they come *(enter **Wise Men**)*; clever chaps who studied the stars. They knew a lot, but one night they were intrigued and puzzled by a bright new star that they hadn't seen before.

(Wise Men can have books and charts on a table that they pore over and murmur together.)

They looked it up and realised that this star indicated a very important event, so important that they couldn't ignore it – the birth of a king. A king in the country where this seemed to be happening must mean Jerusalem, so that was where they headed.

(Wise Men pack up books and set off round the church with gifts.)

Song The First Nowell *(except the last 2 verses) or* The virgin Mary had a baby boy *(except the last verse)*

(Wise Men pause at the back of church when the song stops.)

Wise Man one: *(Calling loudly)* Where is the one who has been born king of the Jews?

Wise Man two: We have seen his star in the east.

Wise Man three: We have come to worship him.

(Sing last verses of song as the Wise Men walk up from the back.)

*(Enter **King Herod** and his **entourage** to stand in the middle, facing the Wise Men, looking threatening.)*

Matthew: King Herod didn't like the look of these strange visitors and he liked their questions about a newborn king even less. His own wise men had looked it up and found a reference to a ruler being born in Bethlehem.

(Herod beckons the Wise Men to him.)

Herod: 'Go and make a careful search for the child. As soon as you find him report to me, so that I too may worship him.'

(Exit Herod and his people.)

Matthew: 'After they heard Herod they went on their way and the star they had seen in the east went ahead of them until it stopped over the place where the child was. When they saw the star stop they were overjoyed.'

(Wise Men continue forward to Mary and Joseph and the baby. They kneel with their gifts.)

'On coming to the house they saw the child with his mother Mary and they bowed down and worshipped him. Then they opened their treasures and presented him with gifts of gold and of incense and of myrrh.'

(Pause.)

I'm glad to be able to tell you that they were warned in a dream not to go back to King Herod, so they returned to their own land by a different route.

(Wise Men move away.)

Isaiah: So there we have it – the prophecies that I heard . . .

Luke: and their fulfilment in the little town of Bethlehem . . .

Matthew: a Saviour – born for you, for me, for all of us, for all time.

Luke: As we said at the beginning, it's quite a story.

Song O come all ye faithful *(3 verses only)*

(During this carol ***Angel Gabriel, shepherds*** *and* ***Wise Men*** *come forward again and form a tableau with Mary and Joseph.)*

Leader: *(Thank yous, acknowledgements and applause as appropriate.)* Let us be quiet for a moment once more as we think about this amazing story – the story of a young family, a birth, a baby. A story of fear, of mystery and strange events; a story of joy, of singing and precious gifts; a story we know well but which always fills us with wonder.

Emmanuel – God with us – the baby who came to make God known to us; to share our lives, our joys and our sorrows; to save us from sin and to lead us to his kingdom one day, to be with him.

Prayers We say together the Lord's Prayer.
Our Father . . .

Son of Mary, Son of God,
we have joined the worship of the angels;
may we never lose that heavenly vision.
Like the shepherds,
we have rejoiced at the news of your birth;
help us to proclaim that message in word and deed,
to your praise and glory.

New Patterns for Worship

And the blessing of God almighty, the Father, the Son, and the Holy Spirit, be among you and remain with you always. Amen.

Song Hark, the herald-angels sing

Christmas Day

Come! Look inside

This is an informal family service for Christmas morning which includes a shortened form of Holy Communion. Have four beautifully wrapped presents on a table at the front. Three of the presents should have rather disappointing things inside, for example a pair of socks, a very dull book, a hideous T-shirt. One should have something beautiful and precious, maybe jewellery or a beautiful vase. Make sure you know which present is which! Have the altar cloth (folded up), one or two candles and some flowers that you can put on the altar or a table. Have two readers and divide up the reading between them as suggested. If wanted, have a box of musical instruments for the children to play with the songs.

Welcome

Hello and a very good morning on this happy day! Let's all greet each other by saying 'Happy Christmas!' Happy Christmas! Yes, it's Christmas Day, so we can light all the candles on our Advent wreath. *(Choose some children to come and light the candles.)*

I bring you good news of great joy:
a Saviour has been born to us.
Alleluia.

Unto us a child is born,
unto us a Son is given.
Alleluia.

He is Christ the Lord. Alleluia.
We worship and adore him.
Alleluia.

New Patterns for Worship

O come, let us adore him. We stand to sing together.

Song O come, all ye faithful *(4 verses)*

Let us be quiet for a moment as we pray.

Father, we rejoice and sing,
for you love us with a great love.
We give thanks to you
for the coming of our Lord Jesus Christ into our world
and into our lives.
Let us enjoy your presence with us,
and the love you offer to us in Jesus our Lord.
Amen.

David Adam

Christmas Day is an exciting and happy day. I hope you have all enjoyed opening some lovely presents. Has anyone brought a present with them that they would like to show us? *(Spend a few minutes talking to children and looking at their presents.)*

(Go over to the presents on the table and look at them.)

Look – there are some presents here too. Don't they look lovely? Aren't they beautifully wrapped? *(Pause and just gaze at them then turn away.)* They look like really lovely presents.

Now we are going to have a reading from the Bible.

Reading *Reader one*

In that region there were shepherds living in the fields, keeping watch over their flock by night. Then the angel of the Lord stood before them, and the glory of the Lord shone round about them, and they were terrified. But the angel said to them–

Reader two

Do not be afraid; for see – I am bringing you good news of great joy for all people; To you is born this day in the city of David a Saviour, who is the Messiah, the Lord. This will be a sign for you; you will find a child wrapped in bands of cloth and lying in a manger.

Reader one

And suddenly there was with the angel a multitude of the heavenly host, praising God and saying–

Reader two

Glory to God in the highest heaven, and on earth peace among those whom he favours!

Reader one

When the angels had left them and gone into heaven, the shepherds said to one another–

Reader two

Let us go now to Bethlehem and see this thing that has taken place, which the Lord has made known to us.

Reader one

So they went with haste and found Mary and Joseph and the child lying in a manger. When they saw this, they made known what had been told them about this child; and all who heard it were amazed at what the shepherds told them.

Reader two

But Mary treasured all these words and pondered them in her heart. The shepherds returned, glorifying and praising God for all they had heard and seen, as it had been told them.

Luke 2:8-20 (NRSV)

(Walk over to look at presents again.) Those presents do look lovely. I love this paper and isn't this ribbon pretty? *(Walk away from them.)* The angels sang. The shepherds sang. Everyone wanted to sing about the Good News of the birth of the baby – Jesus, the Messiah. We're going to sing now. *(Glance at the presents again.)* They do look exciting. *(Turn away from them.)* Would some of you children like to come out and play these instruments as we sing?

Song Come and join the celebration *or* Mary's Boy Child *(or similar)*

Talk *(Walk over to presents.)* These really are lovely presents. I love to see presents under the Christmas tree at home, all beautifully wrapped and with their labels saying who they are for and who they are from. And it's so exciting to wake on Christmas morning and see a bulging stocking or pillowcase by your bed isn't it? I wonder what these presents are? *(Pause and look at them then turn away. Then go back to them.)*

They do look lovely. They do look exciting. But I suppose we won't know what's in them unless we open them. Shall we open them? Oh I don't know. Maybe we won't bother. We could leave them till next week or next month. We could even leave them till next Christmas. Maybe I'll just put them away and forget about them. Or shall I open them? Oh, all right. We'll open them.

Would someone like to come and help me? We'll open this one first . . . Let's see . . . let's see . . . there's lots of tissue and paper. What is it? Oh – socks. Hmm. I didn't really want socks. I've got lots of pairs. Oh well. Let's look at the next present.

What's this? . . . A book. Let's have a look. Hmm. It doesn't look very exciting. It's very long and has very small print and there aren't any pictures. I don't think I'll ever read it.

Let's try this one . . . What have we here? Goodness me! *(Hold up huge, hideous T-shirt.)* I don't think I could go out in this!

Oh dear – what disappointing presents, and they looked so lovely before I opened them. There's one more. Shall we look? Ah – now what is this? Oh look *(hold up beautiful necklace/bracelet/vase)*. Now that is beautiful! What a wonderful present.

We couldn't guess what any of the presents were. They all looked lovely from the outside. We didn't know what was inside until we opened them and looked. The shepherds heard the angel's message. They didn't have to do what the angel told them. They could have stayed on the hillside with their sheep. But they didn't. They went down to Bethlehem. They found the stable and opened the door. They went inside.

The Wise Men saw the star. They didn't have to follow it. No one told them that they must. They could have just read about it in their books and left it at that. But they didn't. They followed the star. They found the place, opened the door and went in.

We don't have to go into the stable either. We can stay outside just listening to the story and the songs. Or we can open the door and go in. Inside we'll find the present from God, there waiting for us.

Some of these presents were a bit disappointing weren't they? Not what was wanted or asked for. We come across many things – and people – day by day that look exciting and tempting but when we try them, when we look at them, open them or go along with them we find that they are nothing. They lead only to disappointment; short-lived thrills leaving emptiness; glitter and glamour that fade away; fair-weather friends who don't stick around.

But not everything or everyone is like that and we can find the best gift of all if we really look and open it; it's the gift that is everlasting, the gift that God sent – his Son. It's a gift not only for Christmas Day but for ever. Let's not leave his gift unopened. Let's receive it, open it, keep it and say 'thank you'.

We bow our heads to pray.

As we open the door of the stable and look inside,
there is Jesus, the baby, lying in a manger.
Let us go to him and kneel in worship,
knowing he is God's Son, born to be our Saviour.
In thanks and praise we accept this gift from our Father God.

In sorrow we acknowledge our weaknesses and failings
and lay them at his feet.
In humility we accept his loving forgiveness.
In love and service we offer him our hearts and our lives.
Amen.

I'm sure that you will all be going back home to a special Christmas dinner. I expect your table will be decorated and all your family will sit round together to enjoy a feast.

We have come here to share God's feast as a church family. We have our dining table here that we will gather round. I hope that you children are a help to your mums on such a busy day. One of the ways you may help is by setting the table. We are going to set this table now and I would like some help to do it while we sing our next song. We have a beautiful tablecloth, some flowers and some candles, and to go in the middle we have a very special silver cup and plate.

We're not going to have roast turkey. The feast we share with Jesus is of bread and wine because that is what he shared with his friends. *(Choose a few children to come out and help prepare the table.)*

Before we sing let us share God's peace.

Unto us a child is born, unto us a son is given
and his name shall be called the Prince of Peace.
The peace of the Lord be always with you.
And also with you.

Common Worship

(During the singing of the carol set the table with the children.)

Song See him lying on a bed of straw

Many of us like to say grace before we begin our meal – thanking God for our food and for his blessings to us. This next prayer is like a grace – a rather long grace that tells a story. If you listen carefully, children, you will hear the story of what Jesus has done for us. There are words for you to join in with too. When I say, 'This is his story,' you reply with, 'This is our song: Hosanna in the highest.'

This is his story.
This is our song:
Hosanna in the highest.

The Lord is here.
His Spirit is with us.

Lift up your hearts.
We lift them to the Lord.

Let us give thanks to the Lord our God.
It is right to give him thanks and praise.

Almighty God, good Father to us all,
your face is turned towards your world.
In love you gave us Jesus your Son
to rescue us from sin and death.

And now we give you thanks,
because by the power of the Holy Spirit
he took our nature upon him
and was born of the Virgin Mary, his mother,
that being himself without sin,
he might make us clean from all sin.

Your Word goes out to call us home
to the city where angels sing your praise.
We join with them in heaven's song:
Holy, holy, holy Lord,
God of power and might,
heaven and earth are full of your glory.
Hosanna in the highest.

Father of all, we give you thanks
for every gift that comes from heaven.
To the darkness Jesus came as your light.
With signs of faith and words of hope
he touched untouchables with love
and washed the guilty clean.

This is his story.
This is our song:
Hosanna in the highest.

The crowds came out to see your Son,
yet at the end they turned on him.
On the night he was betrayed
he came to the table with his friends
to celebrate the freedom of your people.

This is his story.
This is our song:
Hosanna in the highest.

Jesus blessed you, Father, for the food;
he took bread, gave thanks, broke it and said:
'This is my body, given for you all.'
Jesus then gave thanks for the wine;
he took the cup, gave it and said:
'This is my blood, shed for you all
for the forgiveness of sins.
Do this in remembrance of me.'

This is our story.
This is our song:
Hosanna in the highest.

Send your Spirit on us now,
that by these gifts we may feed on Christ
with opened eyes and hearts on fire.

May we and all who share this food
offer ourselves to live for you
and be welcomed at your feast in heaven
where all creation worships you,
Father, Son and Holy Spirit:

Blessing and honour and glory and power
be yours for ever and ever.
Amen.

Common Worship Eucharistic Prayer D

As our Saviour taught us so we pray.
Our Father . . .

We break this bread to share in the body of Christ.
Though we are many, we are one body,
because we all share in the one bread.

Draw near with faith.

(Holy Communion)

Prayer

We praise and thank you, creator God,
for you have not left us alone.
Every year we celebrate your coming as Emmanuel.
Every Eucharist celebrates his death,
in the bread we break and the cup we share,
until that day when we shall see you face to face,
in Jesus Christ our Lord.

New Patterns for Worship

Song Hark, the herald-angels sing

Blessing And the blessing of God almighty, the Father, the Son, and the Holy Spirit, be among you and remain with you always. Amen.

The Word was made flesh and lived among us:
and we have seen his glory.

Go in peace to love and serve the Lord.
In the name of Christ. Amen.

The Sunday after Christmas

When it's all over

The Sunday after Christmas is usually a quiet day. Depending on which day of the week Christmas Day falls it can be as near as the day after, (which probably means there will be very few people there) or almost a week away.

The excitement is over and the visitors may have gone. The day may have a slight feeling of anticlimax. But for Christians it is still a positive time; a time of joy in the message we have heard and a time to move forward into the coming year with renewed hope.

This is a quiet service, a reflection on what has passed and a look at the way ahead. It does not follow the pattern of the previous services. There is no drama or use of props this time but songs, readings (choose three people to be readers) and times for quiet meditation and prayer.

The thoughts and meditations are all based around the words of the song 'Born in the night'. If you have a music group or a soloist they could sing a verse of the song at the beginning of each section. If not the leader can read the words.

Your music group may also like to sing before or after the service. A song such as Matt Redman's 'When the music fades' would be appropriate.

Welcome

When Christmas is over and the festivities done,
it's easy to feel a bit low.
All the presents are opened, the visitors gone;
there's not much left to show.
The tree is dropping needles all over the floor;
it's leftovers for dinner for days.
But it must all mean something, there has to be more –
isn't that what the Good News says?

We probably have come here today for different reasons – it's Sunday and it's what we always do on Sunday morning; maybe we've come to get out of the house – have a bit of peace from all the excitement, the noise and visitors. Perhaps your house – certainly if it's anything like mine – looks a tip and you can't stand it any longer! Maybe we are thinking a bit like that person in the verse – there's got to be more to it than torn wrapping paper, a wilting Christmas tree and leftovers for dinner.

However we are feeling at this moment, Christmas was and is a celebration. So even if we do feel a bit jaded and flat today let us sing in celebration once more of that Good News as we look back over this joyful time.

Song Come on and celebrate *or* Ding, dong merrily on high

Please sit. We listen now to this verse of a song.

Born in the night,
Mary's child,
a long way from your home;
coming in need,
Mary's child,
born in a borrowed room.

(Pause.)

Reading *Reader one*

While they were there, the time came for the baby to be born, and she gave birth to her firstborn, a son. She wrapped him in cloths and placed him in a manger, because there was no room for them in the inn.

Luke 2:6, 7 (NIV)

Meditation

I can picture that scene, the young mother's fear,
and the father's anxious face;
the moments of pain as her time draws near
in that bleak and bare, cold place.
Then the smiles and the joy, a new baby boy,
just like today in any home;
every baby is special, the only one in the world,
but this one – why did he come?

Think back for a few moments on all we have heard over the last two or three weeks – the songs we have sung, the readings we have listened to. Put aside for a moment the celebrations in our homes – the presents, the food, the parties and family gatherings – and picture that scene: the child born in such humble circumstances, in squalor, fear and poverty. Born in the night, Mary's child.

(Pause.)

We have sung the familiar words of carols many times. Yes, they are familiar but they all proclaim the same message of joy and truth. Joy to the world, the Lord is come. *(Pause.)* Hark, the herald-angels sing, glory to the newborn King. *(Pause.)* Unto us a boy is born, King of all creation, came he to a world forlorn, the Lord of every nation. *(Pause.)* Silent night, holy night, Son of God, love's pure light. *(Pause.)*

Let us pray. When I say, 'O come, let us adore him,' please respond with 'Christ the Lord'.

Mary heard the words of the angel and accepted God's will. She responded with humility and with praise. Let us be like Mary as we look in the stable and see her with the Infant King.

O come, let us adore him,
Christ the Lord.

Joseph also heard the words of the angel. In faith and trust he accepted God's will and served God in what he had to do. Let us be like Joseph as we seek to serve our God.

O come, let us adore him,
Christ the Lord.

The shepherds and the Wise Men came in wonder and worship bringing their adoration and their gifts. Let us come too and give what we can – our hearts and our worship.

O come, let us adore him,
Christ the Lord.

Song

Lord Jesus Christ (Living Lord)

Please sit as we listen again.

Clear shining light,
Mary's child,
your face lights up the way;
Light of the world,
Mary's child,
dawn on our darkened day.

Readings

Reader two

In the beginning was the Word, and the Word was with God, and the Word was God. He was with God in the beginning. Through him all things were made; without him nothing was made that has been made. In him was life, and that life was the light of men. The light shines in the darkness, but the darkness has not understood it.

John 1:1-5 (NIV)

Reader three

This is the message we have heard from him and declare to you; God is light; in him there is no darkness at all. If we claim to have fellowship with him yet walk in the darkness, we lie and do not live by the truth. But if we walk in the light, we have fellowship with one another, and the blood of Jesus purifies us from all sin.

1 John 1:5-7 (NIV)

Meditation

Christmas lights – our city streets glisten and sparkle with brightly coloured decorations. Shops and stores shimmer and gleam. We put candles on our tables and lights on our Christmas trees. Churches have candles on the Advent wreath. Many have candlelit carol services.

Why so many lights? Because Jesus is the Light of the World. He comes to bring light into the darkness – the darkness of a sinful world, a world of conflict, of pain, suffering and sorrow. And he comes to bring light into the dark shadows of our own lives. *(Pause.)*

Your face lights up the way – dawn on our darkened day. Let us pray.

Come, my Lord,
my light, my way;
come my lantern,
night and day,
come healer,
make me whole.
Come, my Saviour,
protect my soul;
come my king,
enter my heart;
come Prince of Peace,
and never depart.

David Adam

Song All earth was dark (Lights to the world) *or* Thou, whose almighty word

Please sit as we listen again.

Truth of our life,
Mary's child,
you tell us God is good;
prove it is true,
Mary's child.
Go to your cross of wood.

Readings *Reader one*

For God so loved the world that he gave his one and only Son that whoever believes in him should not perish but have eternal life. For God did not send his Son into the world to condemn the world, but to save the world through him.

John 3:16, 17 (NIV)

Reader two

When they came to the place called 'The Skull', there they crucified him, along with the criminals – one on his right, the other on his left. Jesus said, 'Father, forgive them for they do not know what they are doing.'

Luke 23:33, 34 (NIV)

Meditation

In the darkness of the stable,
on a lonely night,
a shadow fell across the floor
in beams of silver light.
It was the shadow of a cross,
the shadow of a cross;
a mark of suffering and sorrow,
that night, but waiting for tomorrow.

In the early hours of morning,
as the baby slept,
Mary stood outside the door,
and as she prayed she wept.
She saw the shadow of a cross,
the shadow of a cross;
that pierced her loving heart with sorrow,
that night, but waiting for tomorrow.

When our hearts are filled with darkness
through the lonely night,
we lift our eyes and looking upward
see the dawning light;
in the shadow of the cross,
the shadow of a cross,
the light of love ends all our sorrow
and hope shines brightly for tomorrow.

Let us pray.

Lord Jesus Christ,
you humbled yourself in taking the form of a servant,
and in obedience died on the cross for our salvation;
give us the mind to follow you
and to proclaim you as Lord and King,
to the glory of God the Father.

Common Worship

Song From heaven you came (The Servant King)

We listen to the final verse.

Hope of the world,
Mary's child,
you're coming soon to reign;
King of the earth,
Mary's child,
walk in our streets again.

Reading *Reader three*
How beautiful on the mountains
are the feet of those who bring good news,
who proclaim peace,
who bring good tidings,
who proclaim salvation,
who say to Zion, 'Your God reigns!'
Listen! Your watchmen lift up their voices;
together they shout for joy.
The Lord will lay bare his holy arm
in the sight of all nations,
and all the ends of the earth
will see the salvation of our God.
Isaiah 52:7, 8, 10 (NIV)

Meditation 'Behold, I am coming soon! I am the Alpha and Omega, the First and the Last, the Beginning and the End.'

(Pause.)

At the start of Advent we thought not only about the coming of the baby Jesus at Christmas but also of his second coming – the glorious day when Jesus Christ will come in splendour and majesty to reign as King; the day when 'the hope of the world will walk in our streets again'.

(Pause.)

Then I saw a new heaven and a new earth – God himself will be with them . . . He will wipe away every tear from their eyes. There will be no more death or mourning or crying or pain. For the old order of things has passed away.

(Pause.)

Let us pray. When I say, 'Maranatha' – the Aramaic word meaning 'Our Lord, come' – please respond with 'Amen. Come, Lord Jesus'.

In joyful expectation of his coming we pray to Jesus saying,
Maranatha.
Amen. Come, Lord Jesus.

Come to your Church as Lord and judge.
We pray for . . .
Help us to live in the light of your coming
and give us a longing for your kingdom.

Maranatha.
Amen. Come, Lord Jesus.

Come to your world as King of the nations.
We pray for . . .
Before you, rulers will stand silent.

Maranatha.
Amen. Come, Lord Jesus.

Come to your people with a message of victory and peace.
We pray for . . .
Give us the victory over death, temptation and evil.

Maranatha.
Amen. Come, Lord Jesus.

Come to us as Saviour and Comforter.
We pray for . . .
Break into our lives,
where we struggle with sickness and distress,
and set us free to serve you for ever.

Maranatha.
Amen. Come, Lord Jesus.

Come to us from heaven, Lord Jesus,
with power and great glory.
Lift us up to meet you, with all your saints and angels,
to live with you for ever.

Maranatha.
Amen. Come, Lord Jesus.

New Patterns for Worship

We say together the Lord's Prayer.
Our Father . . .

Song How lovely on the mountains (Our God reigns) *or* I cannot tell *or* The splendour of the King

Blessing Now may the Lord of peace himself
give you peace at all times and in every way.
The Lord be with you all.
New Patterns for Worship

And the blessing of God almighty, the Father, the Son, and the Holy Spirit, be among you and remain with you always. Amen.

Epiphany

Guiding lights

For the children's activity you will need:

- three small bags of chocolate gold-wrapped coins hidden in and around the church
- an envelope containing a set of simple directions to one hiding place
- an envelope containing a diagram or map to another hiding place
- a scarf in a bag or packet and secret instructions in an envelope

For the talk you will need a crown, a star and a globe. Choose three people for the Bible readings.

Welcome

Welcome to our church on Epiphany Sunday. This day marks the end of the season that has taken us from Advent to Christmas and through to Epiphany. January 6th is the official feast day of Epiphany – the twelfth day after Christmas Day. We all know the song 'The twelve days of Christmas' I'm sure. On this day we do think about some Christmas gifts – though not quite as many as in that song and not quite as peculiar either! Some of those gifts were very strange – Lords a-leaping, ladies dancing, swans a-swimming and all sorts of other odd things; all quite useless and pointless.

The gifts we hear about today are quite different. They are very precious and full of rich meaning. We begin by singing an Epiphany hymn.

Song Brightest and best of the sons of the morning *or* As with gladness men of old

First of all we come to God in prayer. As the Christmas season comes to a close we think of all that we have heard and all that we have sung about. We thank God for the holiday we have enjoyed, the presents we have received, the love that we have shared. But we know that there have been times when we have failed him in some way. We come now to confess our failure to God and to ask his forgiveness.

Confession Christ came in humility to share our lives:
forgive our pride.
Lord have mercy.
Lord have mercy.

Christ came with good news for all people:
forgive our silence.
Christ have mercy.
Christ have mercy.

Christ came in love to a world of suffering:
forgive our self-centredness.
Lord have mercy.
Lord have mercy.

New Patterns for Worship

Absolution May the God of all healing and forgiveness
draw *us* to himself,
and cleanse *us* from all our sins
that *we* may behold the glory of his Son,
the Word made flesh,
Jesus Christ our Lord.
Amen.

New Patterns for Worship

Activity Has anybody read *Treasure Island*? It's a great story about finding buried treasure. There's a map to follow and a cross that marks the place on the island where the treasure is hidden. There are goodies and baddies, heroes and villains, and plenty of adventure, excitement and danger before the treasure is found.

In church today there are some pieces of hidden treasure! It's not quite such valuable treasure as might be found in a story I'm afraid but it's still got to be found.

There are three lots of treasure and three different ways to find them. Here are some envelopes. We'll open them and see if they tell us what to do. *(Open the envelope with the written directions in it. Choose a couple of children to come out and read them.)*

Now let's see what we've got. It's a list of directions. Right, we need to read them and do what it says.

(Read out the directions for the children to follow, for example, start at the pulpit, take 10 paces to the right, turn left, take 10 more paces and so on with more directions, until they find the 'treasure'.)

Well done! That wasn't too hard was it? Let's have a look in the next envelope. *(Choose a couple more children.)*

It's a diagram – a kind of map. Look, X marks the spot where the treasure will be. It says 'you are here' at this arrow so then you have to follow the map and see if you can find your way. Off you go.

(Children use map to find treasure.)

You've found it! Well done. Now this last envelope has a packet with it. What's in the packet? A scarf! Let me open the envelope and see what it says. *(Read it inaudibly to yourself.)* Oh – this is a bit different and could be a bit tricky.

I need two people who are good friends. *(Teenagers would be best for this.)* Now, do you two trust each other? Are you good friends? I'm going to blindfold one of you with this scarf. Now I'm going to show your friend this letter marked 'secret' which says where the treasure is hidden and *(he)* is going to direct you there by telling you where to go. Off you go.

(Friend instructs, for example, walk forward, stop, turn right, walk forward, stop, and so on until they get to the 'treasure'.)

(Remove blindfold.) Well done! That wasn't easy was it? You really had to trust your friend. Were you afraid that you might bump into something and hurt yourself?

There are many different ways to show us how to get to somewhere we want to be or to something we want to find. We can use maps. Someone can tell us the route or write it down for us. You can download instructions on your computer. And of course now we have satnav. Who has a satnav in their car? Are they always foolproof I wonder? Can we trust them like *(name)* had to trust *(his)* friend?

Many years ago ships would navigate by the stars. The Wise Men followed a star until they found what they were looking for. In a moment, after we have sung our next carol *(hymn)*, we will hear some of their story.

Song We three kings *or* Hail to the Lord's anointed

In the weeks of Advent we heard words from the prophets foretelling the birth of Jesus and also of his coming again. Listen to these verses from Isaiah and from one of the psalms.

Readings *Reader one*

Arise, shine, for your light has come,
and the glory of the Lord has risen upon you.
For darkness shall cover the earth
and thick darkness the peoples;
but the Lord will arise upon you,
and his glory will appear over you.
Nations will come to your light,

and kings to the brightness of the dawn . . .
And those from Sheba shall come.
They shall bring gold and frankincense,
and shall proclaim the praise of the Lord.

Isaiah 60:1-3, 6b (NRSV)

Reader two

May the kings of Tarshish and of the isles render him tribute,
may the kings of Sheba and Seba bring gifts.
May all kings fall down before him,
all nations give him service . . .
Long may he live!
May gold of Sheba be given to him . . .
Blessed be his glorious name forever;
may his glory fill the whole earth.

Psalm 72:10, 11, 15a, 19a (NRSV)

So now we hear about those kings.

Reader three

After Jesus was born in Bethlehem in Judea, during the time of King Herod, Magi from the east came to Jerusalem and asked, 'Where is the one who has been born king of the Jews? We saw his star in the east and have come to worship him.'

. . . they went on their way, and the star they had seen in the east went ahead of them until it stopped over the place where the child was. When they saw the star, they were overjoyed. On coming to the house, they saw the child with his mother Mary, and they bowed down and worshipped him. Then they opened their treasures and presented him with gifts of gold and of incense and of myrrh.

Matthew 2:1, 2, 9-11 (NIV)

The Wise Men were the first people from other countries to worship Jesus. We sing in worship now.

Song Come, now is the time to worship *or* O worship the Lord in the beauty of holiness

Talk *(This is an illustration from my own experience that you can use if you wish, or use your own similar anecdote.)*

I have sometimes stayed in Dartmouth on holiday. It's a beautiful place – I expect many of you may know it – where the River Dart flows into the sea. There is a lively harbour full of yachts, pleasure boats for cruising up and down as well as some fishing boats and working boats. There are Royal Navy training boats too from the college there in Dartmouth. You can sit for ages on the harbour side watching the boats coming and going. There's never a dull moment.

On this particular occasion we were interested to see a huge private yacht, white and gleaming, moored in the centre of the harbour. It looked to be the height of luxury. Everyone was fascinated and gazed at it in admiration. The gossip was that it belonged to a multimillionaire from South America.

It was there for a couple of days. You could catch a glimpse of some of the smartly dressed crew and see the lights twinkling at night. We happened to be down by the water when it was getting ready to leave. As we watched we saw a very small boat come alongside the yacht. It looked tiny in comparison. It chugged along to the front of the yacht and went ahead as the yacht slowly began to move. The little boat knew precisely the way to go to take it on the right course, away from shallow water, keeping in the middle and guiding it safely out to sea. The tiny pilot boat led the enormous yacht to safety. The yacht couldn't have managed without it.

(Hold up the crown.) The Wise Men needed a guide for their long journey. Their guide was a star. 'We saw his star in the east and have come to worship him.' We often talk about stars, in many different contexts. There's the 'star of the show' – the person

who is most important or well-known in a play or musical. A 'star-studded cast' would include lots of famous people. There are pop stars, sports stars, opera stars, actors and many other celebrities – all stars in their own field. You might say 'you're a star' to a child who has done well. Young children all know 'Twinkle, twinkle little star'. *(If you have a lot of young children in church, and it is appropriate, sing the nursery rhyme at this point.)*

On a clear night we can look up and see the stars in the sky that seem to twinkle as they shine. We can pick out different constellations – the Plough, the Great Bear and others. The North Star has often been used as a guide for travellers and explorers.

The Wise Men understood the stars. They searched for meaning in them. In this particular star they discovered something new and important and they realised that this was of huge significance and they had to act upon it. They didn't just say 'well, fancy that' and put their books away. They did something about it. They followed the star until they found what they were looking for, until they understood what it meant.

There are many things that sparkle and dazzle; many stars to follow and to lead us this way and that way and quite often the wrong way. This one guiding star led the Wise Men to the right place. They had taken their precious gifts, treasures fit for a king, and they found their treasure, a precious gift from God to them. It is our treasure too; God's gift to us – his Son.

Jesus said 'Where your treasure is, there will your heart be.' Jesus can be our star and guide us along the way. He can be like that pilot boat leading the yacht safely on its way.

(Hold up the crown.) Some people like to call the Wise Men kings. We don't know very much about them. Different traditions have grown up over the years. Some say their names were Caspar, Melchior and Balthazar but we don't really know. We do know that they were knowledgeable about the stars and planets. We know they were well educated. We know they must have been wealthy and important, because of the richness of their gifts. They probably weren't kings but they came to find a king. The most important king in the account is the one that is newborn – the infant Jesus.

The earthly King Herod was frightened and angry at the thought of another king. He didn't understand that Jesus is the King who will one day rule heaven and earth. The Wise Men were the first to know about this kingship – and they came from another country. They weren't Jews waiting for their Messiah. They made the discovery seemingly by chance when they weren't really looking. Their message tells the world that Jesus has come for everyone.

(Hold up the globe.) That star in the east shone for all people, for all time. It stopped over the place where there was a much brighter light – the Light of the World. 'Arise, shine, for your light has come,' said Isaiah. The word 'epiphany' means 'showing' or 'manifestation'. The truth has been shown to us. We sometimes say 'oh, the light has dawned' when we suddenly understand something. It's as if someone has switched on the light in a dark room and we can see. Or it's like when we took the blindfold off *(name). (He'd)* been in the dark but then *(he)* could see.

We can understand what happened. The Wise Men have shown us by following that star. Epiphany marks the end of the Christmas season but it is not the end. It's the beginning. It falls at the beginning of a new year when we may be unsure of what lies ahead. Epiphany speaks to us of light, of kingship and of a message for the whole world.

In the days ahead let Jesus be our guiding light, the star to follow and the pilot to lead us safely on our way until he brings us home to that heavenly harbour.

Earlier in the service, when our young friends were looking for the treasure here in church, some of them found the way to go by reading directions or following a map. We have the Bible. It gives us instructions and teaches us. But most of all we have a friend we can trust to lead us and guide us. The Wise Men trusted the star. They couldn't make it on their own. *(Name)* had to trust *(his)* friend when *(he)* was blindfolded to tell *(him)* the way to go. *(He)* couldn't make it on *(his)* own. The enormous yacht trusted the tiny pilot boat. In spite of its luxury, its size and hi-tech equipment, it couldn't make it on its own. We can't make it on our own.

Prayers

Let us pray.

The special prayer for Epiphany:

O God,
who by the leading of the star
manifested your only Son to the peoples of the earth:
mercifully grant that we who know you now by faith,
may at last behold your glory face to face;
through Jesus Christ our Lord,
who is alive and reigns with you,
in the unity of the Holy Spirit,
one God, now and for ever.

Common Worship

The Wise Men came from other lands to worship the newborn King. Simeon spoke of a light to lighten the Gentiles. The light that Jesus brings is for everyone, everywhere. So we pray for the mission of the Church.

We think of the Church worldwide and pray for . . .

We think of the Church in this our country and pray for . . .

We think of the Church in this community and pray for . . .

At the end of the Christmas season and the start of a new year we look to Jesus to guide us in the days ahead.

When this world is as dark as night,
you are the One we call the light.
When we are tempted to go astray,
you are the One we call the way.
When we are falling in the strife,
you are the One who is the life.
When troubles to our lives bring harm,
you are the One who brings us calm.

David Adam

We say together the prayer that Jesus taught us.
Our Father . . .

Statement of faith

We stand to declare what we believe.

Though he was divine,
he did not cling to equality with God,
but made himself nothing.
Taking the form of a slave,
he was born in human likeness.
He humbled himself
and was obedient to death,
even the death on a cross.
Therefore God has raised him on high,
and given him the name above every name;
that at the name of Jesus
every knee should bow,
and every voice proclaim that Jesus Christ is Lord,
to the glory of God the Father.
Amen.

New Patterns for Worship

Song

Thou, whose almighty word *or* Lord, the light of your love (Shine, Jesus, shine)

Blessing

When they saw the star they were overjoyed. May we, too, be filled with joy and seek to share this joy with others. And the blessing of God almighty, the Father, the Son, and the Holy Spirit, be among you and remain with you always. Amen.

Let us go in peace.
We go into the world
to walk in God's light,
to rejoice in God's love
and to reflect God's glory.
Amen.

New Patterns for Worship